REVERSE THE CURSE

Break free. Live blessed.

REVERSE THE CURSE

Break free. Live blessed.

YOLANDA LEWIS
Garrin J. Mason
Tanya O'Brien
Jason LaPlanche
Lakeisha S. Powe

Extreme Overflow Publishing
A brand of Extreme Overflow Enterprises, Inc
P.O. Box 1184
Grayson, GA 30017
www.extremeoverflow.com
info@extreme-overflow-enterprises.com

Library of Congress Catalog-in-Publication Data is available for this title.

ISBN: 978-0-9976256-7-7 (Printed)
ISBN: 978-0-9976256-8-4 (EBook)

Printed in the United States of America

TABLE OF CONTENTS

INTRODUCTION

What is stopping you from doing better with your life? Be honest. What do you think is keeping you from living the life you've always dreamed of? Whose fault is it?

You may hear some people blame society, technology or culture. Others will blame their peers, but very few will look at their self as the block that is preventing an enjoyable life. Without accountability it is impossible to truly take authority and empower your life. In other words, without accountability you become like a shark with no teeth; powerless, until you are accountable to your part. To be accountable to your part you have to first be responsible for your behavior. When you are responsible for your own behavior, then you have the power to change it.

Experiments show that a traumatic event could affect the DNA in sperm and alter the brains behavior of subsequent generations (Gallagher, 2013). According to a neuroscience study that trained mice to avoid a smell, the mice passed their aversion of this scent on to their "grandchildren." The study revealed that a section of the DNA responsible for sensitivity to that particular scent was made more active in the mice's sperm. They also noticed changes in the brain structure as well.

The findings within this study provide evidence that a person's environment and experiences can affect an individual's genetics, and in turn can be passed on to the next generation. The formal term for this process is called "Transgenerational epigenetic inheritance."

People tend to think a generational curse; or a Transgenerational epigenetic inheritance, is limited to behaviors of addiction to drugs and alcohol. The reality is these addictions are possibly mere subsets of a core issue. But what if a generational curse could also be defined by poor eating habits, phobias, anxiety or depression?

From the aforementioned study, scientists have concluded that it is high time for public health researchers to take a deeper look at Transgenerational responses and take them more seriously. Like the revelation of these scientists, churches, communities and the like must take the tactics of the devil more seriously as well; he is real and he is destroying many families.

What has happened to society as a whole is a reflection of our neglect as a people; ignoring the root of issues. If in fact society continues to ignore and not teach the truth about personal identity, about the God ordained power we hold as people, and about how to address these familiar familial behavioral patterns, our culture is doomed. You will find more and more people falling face first into every trick, plot and plan Satan sets before them; giving him access to their life and robbing them of the peace God intended for his people to posses.

Since there is nothing new under the sun, Satan can only latch on to what is familiar; tempting you with the same. The biggest deception of a generational curse is to get you to believe it doesn't exist. If you don't believe it exists you'll do nothing to change the pattern. Then it continues and the gift, promise and purpose die with the destruction of your lineage; a legacy destroyed.

What are you passing down to the next generation by not confronting your own 'demons?' What weapons are you giving the next generation to fight against those familiar behaviors that have become spiritual strongholds in your family? When does it stop? Will it be with you?

Taking responsibility for your own behavior is the first step toward enjoying life as it was meant to be. While it seems simple enough, many find themselves avoiding personal responsibility because it can drudge up things you thought were gone. Things you thought were out of sight and out of mind. Feelings and emotions you ignored and swept under the rug. It can be painful confronting challenges when you are the one left picking up the pieces. Sometimes issues can run so deep that your neglect awakened turns numb with preoccupations of pleasure. Don't worry; you're not alone in looking for ways to ease the pain. I too was deceived and eased my pain by ignoring my issues; a very familiar familial coping pattern.

I hated my past; my innocence was stolen from me through sexual abuse beginning at the tender age of three. A perverted relationship was all I knew how to have after that and was the onset of a lost personal identity. I was angry about it all; why me, how come no one saved me, why three years old, and why did I feel like it was my fault?

The anger I experienced and often suppressed, was the open door to many dead relationships, passive aggressiveness, loneliness, crying myself to sleep, suicidal thoughts and attempts and the weight of countless secrets. Let me tell you. Satan has no respect of persons. He doesn't care how old you are, what race you are, or how much money you were or were not born into. He will reach as far back as possible to connect you to whatever is familiar and destroy, distract and deter you from realizing the potential your destiny holds. People think bad things only happen to people who deserve it; not true.

I grew up with two wonderful parents. They both worked hard and created the best life they possibly could for me and my siblings. Home was always good and was always safe. My parents sought out to give us a different life than they had experienced. We went to church every Sunday, Wednesday and Saturday; I grew up in church.

At church, I sang in the choir, served on the usher board, taught Sunday school and went on to lead many different auxiliaries serving in various capacities. I knew church and was convinced that also meant I knew God.

Church life was busy. There were always things going on. It seemed like the perfect place to hide what I was really going through inside. With everyone so busy, I felt that no one would take the time to notice my anger or sadness. I did my best to make sure that was true.

I stayed busy in the church and often hid my true emotions behind my smile. I felt that as long as I sang on key and answered every bible question correctly, no one would ask if anything was wrong. Not even my parents.

I was smart and responsible. I did what I was supposed to do; it was my rhythm, pain was my music. The reality was I knew church but I didn't have the heart to get to know God. I felt I had too many secrets. I felt if He knew those secrets He'd turn me away for sure. There were times in service I felt a drawing to let go, but I quickly grieved the moment. I was convinced that there was no way God wanted or was interested in what was in my heart. I couldn't trust Him to find out because I didn't know how to trust; I didn't trust anyone. So I committed myself to church and all that entailed while life went on.

After my first attempt at attending college, I told my parents about my trauma. They were devastated, but I couldn't hold it in any longer; it was killing me and it was the reason, "why," to so many things wrong in my life.

Eventually I got married to a man who found a way to penetrate my heart. God used him to teach me how to love, purely. Soon after we were married we moved away. When we moved away, that was when I was confronted with all that had grown toxic within me. That was when change started happening. I hurt, grieved, prayed, fasted, was counseled, started journaling, and read a lot of books trying to get better. That was when I really got to know God for myself, not just the scriptures I had memorized from church.

Chains of guilt, shame, low self esteem, and wanting to take my own life were broken. While I had heard His voice before, this was the first time I could feel God's hand of love hold my heart and shower love all over my life.

As time progressed, I was renewed, restored and given peace in my heart. It was refreshing to be free. I learned that God loved me more than any sin I had ever committed. I learned that all while I didn't know Him, He knew me and never gave up on me, never lost hope and never wanted bad for my life. He had choice blessings just for me, no matter how terrible of a start my life had or how big of a mistake I made or how badly I had ruined relationships. He was faithful and his mercy for my soul everlasting. It was then that I learned that I could trust him, with my whole heart.

At no point during that process was it easy, nor was it short. During that time I cried many nights and was frustrated often with what seemed like a lack of progress. But I kept praying and reaching for more of God. As I did, He began to show me more of me; even down to revealing the areas of spiritual bondage connected to my family; my family, my husband's family and our children.

Every experience in your life and those of your forefathers are not gone, even if they are forgotten. They become a part of the molecular residue that develops your genetics; alongside the spiritual, psychological and behavioral tendencies that are inherited. This means that you might not only look like your grandmother, or pray like your grandmother, but you very well may have been predisposed to her negative thinking, unless you decide to do something different.

Research has demonstrated that as environmental factors change the molecular structure on a behavioral level, they also transform on a cognitive level. Meaning there is a chemical response that happens in your brain when you make a choice to change your behavior. From a biological perspective, your choice to actually change the way you do things can alter the very strand of your DNA (Hurley, 2015). It can mutate the DNA to code or recode itself and thereby pass on a new way of thinking; a new way of living out your family legacy. While Satan may have convinced you that you can never change, God designed you amazing; He does all things well and the truth is you possess the power to change. Therefore if you can find a way to do something different; change your environment, change how things have always been done in your family, then you can break the pattern. You can reverse the curse.

As you read this book, know that timing matters. Whether you are a parent who in your heart knows you are mistreating your children or if you are an adult or teen who was mistreated in your childhood, there is no better time than the present to change forward. What you do today is more likely to affect the epigenome of your brain far more strongly than you waiting on someone else in your family lineage to do it. Science is just catching up to the life God intended for all of us to experience in Him; abundant life.

Abundant life means freedom. Right now, in this moment, God is offering you freedom. Wouldn't you like to be free from the pain of rape, abandonments, and the cheated childhoods of your ancestors?

You or your parents may have made some bad decisions in life or experienced terrible circumstances. That's ok. If you are reading this book, you have the opportunity to change the very course of your lineage and recreate an amazing legacy.

It is my hope that you will explore through self reflection, spiritual reformation and mind transformation a sense of purpose, proclamation and power to reverse the curse(s) that may be keeping you from living the best life God has in store for you.

SCARRED

Garrin J. Mason

"Understand that the curse doesn't start with you; the seed has already been planted. Until you address it, it is manifesting and grows stronger and stronger."

First off, my name is Garrin Jaton Mason. I was born in Nashville, Tennessee in the year of 1983. I was the last child of four siblings; I have two older sisters and one older brother. My mom raised us all and without help from either one of our fathers. My two oldest sisters have the same father but my brother and I have different fathers. Even though my mom did it all by herself, we still lived a normal life. When I say normal, I mean 'not poor.' Did we have hard times? Yes, but we never went through anything severe. Even still, how I grew up as a kid made me who I am today and who I am today is not how I use to be.

THE CURSE
From the beginning of time, or life as I've seen it, the lives of men and women have been conflicted. Families across

the world seem to be stereotyped, racially profiled, targeted and broken. The world teaches that, "you are what you see." This is one of the statements that had a major impact on my life. Whenever you're in an environment where all you hear and see is negativity or when you've been raised in a certain type of lifestyle, you will be prone to do what you see and hear. It all starts to feel and be normal. All you know is what you see in front of you. Drugs, alcohol, seeing different men or women pass through, crime, and all types of chaos become the norm. From birth this life may have been all you have ever seen. You may even feel cursed by the history of not knowing anything different. That was me.

When I really started to know and realize what was happening and what I was doing to myself physically and mentally, I knew I needed to break free from two generations of curses. It happened slowly but it was happening because I was determined to break this cycle.

HISTORY

Understand that the curse doesn't start with you; the seed has already been planted. Until you address it, it is manifesting and grows stronger and stronger.

My only knowledge of my family history comes from what "he says, she says." I have no solid background of who my ancestors are to include my grandfathers and grandmothers from my dad side of the family; that's a curse by itself. I was raised by my mother who was a single parent. She was also raised in a single parented home by her mother; my grandmother. My grandmother died when I was only seven years young and my grandfather was never talked about. I found out later in life that my grandfather died when my mother was a kid. My father, pops, daddy, dad, or whatever you want to call him, I never knew much about. The only information I had on my pops growing up was a name; Simon Weaver.

I didn't meet my father until I was nineteen years old and right to this day I still don't know my pops. I met my half sisters before I met my own dad. I have a half brother that died before we could meet, we were the same age but I was six months older. The day we were supposed to have met, we didn't get the chance to. He died two weeks later from a gunshot wound. After meeting my pops for the first time, we met up again. This was the point I started to realize there had to be a curse in effect.

At the point in my life when I was about to meet my dad again, it was normal for me to "not know" why he wasn't there. I thought it was normal to not have a dad. You'd think any normal kid would have questions for their dad and want to be around their dad to build a relationship, but not me. My curse was already too deep and rooted. Everybody around me didn't have their dads.

My grandmother had ten children and even though I know all of my uncles and aunts, I have never been told a story about their dads. What I learned later on was that their father's were either part time, present but not really or not present. Looking back I know that this whole thing about 'not knowing' was a curse way deeper than me. There were generations of "not having," and "not knowing." The reality is I was conceived in a curse.

Not having a father figure caused me major issues that I couldn't even try to understand. All I knew was my mom who was working hard to make sure we were straight. When I had the chance to know my pops, I just couldn't do it. It was hard to open up and receive him as my dad. Who knows what knowing him could have led to. Maybe it could have led to my destruction as a father. That is if I

5

didn't have the courage to do something different about my life.

MY CURSE

I was born into this world cursed from a family tree of missing fathers being in the lives of their children consistently. How is it possible to have an entire family with no men in anyone's life consistently? It would be easy to believe that it was just me that was cursed to live without a father figure in my life, but now I know, I was just one of the many people who grew up without a relationship with their father.

One thing that I know for sure had the most impact on me, was watching my mom do it all by herself; she was an independent woman. I had it in my mind that once I got older I was going to do things "my way." I was determined to be independent.

From the start I never had positive guidance from any father figure to tell me otherwise. I don't take anything from my mom about raising me because she did what she had to do and I'll say she did a perfect job. Raising a boy to be a man is hard if you're not a man. My mom taught me how to live life respectfully but from a woman's perspective. My mom did a great job but who knows where I would've been if my pops was around. I grew up seeing things that a four, five, or six year old should never see. I saw a lot because I'm the baby of the family and all my siblings are pretty much older than me by double digits except my brother. He's nine years older.

My brother had the most influence on me because we were the closest in age so I was around him the most. I watched what he was doing and early on I knew I wanted in. My mom did it all, so in my eyes, I thought doing it all was the way things were supposed to be done. Just like my momma, I had a "by any means necessary" attitude. By any means necessary I was going to get me some money and it didn't matter if it was made through illegal avenues. That was normal. I had seen it all my life. I was surrounded by it. I was born into it. I felt like it was my calling, but really it was all a part of the curse.

My first time doing anything illegal was smoking weed and I was only thirteen years old when I did it. I thought I was the only, coolest, slickest, teenager doing it. Marijuana turned me into a straight up rebel. I thought I knew all about life; no one could tell me anything. I was close to my mom and always wanted to tell her everything that was going on with me but I thought she wouldn't understand so I kept my extracurricular life away from her. I'm pretty sure having pops around would've definitely made me feel different about saying something or even changed my mind about getting into that life.

After my first time smoking I started to smoke on a regular basis. Not every single day but a lot for a thirteen year old. For most people smoking weed is a gateway to do worse drugs...not me. For me, it led to something far more sinister than that. Smoking weed attacked and altered my mind so bad that it led me to believe that I could be the best, most successful drug dealer on earth. Selling drugs is what led me to my doom. Not only was I using drugs and destroying my own mind, I was also enabling other people to destroy their lives by selling them drugs. I was killing two birds with one stone. That's how messed up my thoughts were. See how the curse works? It was working double time to destroy me and everything around me. From the time of my birth, the curse was already marked carving out my life through my ancestry. It was lurking throughout my whole family destroying everything around them and now it was my turn. The curse was a familiar way of life. All that was left to do now was for me to spark it back up. With just a simple thought that popped in my head, "do it all," I decided that is what I was going to do. My mom did it all, why couldn't I "do it all?" My do it all attitude was a little different though. I wanted to sell all types of drugs that could get me money. More like sell it all. If there was an addiction for it, I wanted to sell it.

I was fourteen when I sold my first drug; it was a heroin substitute in a yellow pill form that street hustlers called "beans." The pharmaceutical term is K-4 or Dilaudid. I sold one pill for sixty dollars and after that it was no turning back. I was on my way to the top of the drug chain; at least I thought I was. I wanted to sell drugs full time and drop out of school but I knew if I dropped out of school, my mom would find out. Getting caught was not an option; caught by my mom or the law. Especially my mom; my mother didn't play any games when it came to selling drugs. She kicked my brother out of the house when she found out he was doing it. So, getting caught was not an option.

My high school bus stop was the highest drug trafficking area in my neighborhood. What a coincidence right? I was able to sell my K-4's right where my bus stopped before I went to school. It was easy. That curse seemed to work so good in my favor that I know for sure it was the devil himself helping me to destroy "me." If there was no more me, who would carry on the curse?

I was able to sell drugs undetected from my mother and the law without any interference. I would leave the house thirty minutes to an hour before my bus arrived so I could sell most of what I had. Some days the money would come so rapid that I would be able to sell twenty to thirty pills at twenty dollars apiece.

For a young teenager that age is a lot of money. Imagine selling fifty or a hundred pills a day at twenty dollars apiece, big bucks right? The most I sold in a day was fifty-five pills, not all at once but some in the morning and some after school. The money would come so fast sometimes; I couldn't even count it between the times of dealing with another customer. Making all this money had me hooked, I wanted to sell drugs all my life.

All my dreams of being a basketball star or a football star went away. They didn't go away slowly either, they went away as fast as a train passing by. I started dreaming of being a street legend. I was being lead to a road where I was about to be another statistic, another misguided black kid, another black juvenile delinquent, another black prisoner. The irony of the situation is that there was nobody to blame. History repeats itself. Sometimes the individuals living it barely have a clue as to what is going on. There was a time when I didn't know what was going on, but when I found out, I was determined to undo what was happening to me.

I continued to sell drugs all the way through my teenage years but stopped selling the pharmaceutical drug to sell another; crack cocaine. After a few months of being kicked out of high school my freshman year, I became a full fledge dope man; still a teenager though. It was time to switch hustles anyway because it was becoming too dangerous to sell pills. All of my friends were starting to go to juvenile and jail because the heroin addicts would do anything for a fix or freedom. They even became confidential informants (C.I.) for the police and vice squad. I started selling crack cocaine to stay off the radar from cops. Boy was I blinded!

Little did I know back then, a drug is a drug. It didn't matter what drug you were selling. When you got caught, you were still going to jail. Key words, "when you got caught" and not "if you get caught."

In the life I was living, it was never the "if factor." It was always just a matter of time. Trust me when I say, time wasn't on my side. The curse that was set upon my family was working. Throughout my three years of selling drugs as a teenager, I never went to juvenile for selling drugs and that's what I was doing the most. I did go to juvenile, but for small stuff like, trespassing, being out passed curfew, or loitering during school hours, things of that nature. I once went to juvenile for something serious. I ended up on probation as a teenager but still it wasn't drug related. Things started to get more serious once I turned eighteen. The minute a person turns the big 1-8, they are considered an adult, "grown" as I would say. Grown is how I acted and believe me, grown is how I was treated.

I turned eighteen in January and at the end of May I was in jail. Yes, I said it, jail! No one is invincible; not even me. I thought I could break the law forever and not have any consequences. I went from fourteen to seventeen without any major setbacks. Then all of a sudden I was in jail. But that didn't stop me. I went a few years without getting caught the first time so who's to say I'll get caught faster than the first time? My curse was speaking to me. I was oblivious to the tricks it played on my mind; it was trying to destroy me and whatever future I had left to live. Sad to say but I spent all of my adult years in and out of jail or prison, mostly in. The longest I stayed free was two years straight. Honestly I don't know how that happened.

By this point I was ten times worse than before. I picked up a habit with guns, and I would carry my gun(s) everywhere I went. Corner store, grocery store, youth centers, the mall, it didn't matter. If I could have it with me at the place I was at, then my gun was with me. During this time I also started robbing folks for money. I started to do it often, so often that I slowed down selling drugs.

Robbing was something easy that I could get away with, because the people I was robbing couldn't go to the police. They were just like me, thugs! And thugs don't call the police. Truth be told, I really didn't like robbing, robbing was weak and easy. I was a drug dealer, a dope boy. My ace, right hand man, my pat'na (partner), brother from another, is who liked to rob. He lived for it and hanging with him on a daily is how I picked up the art of robbing. Being a dope boy was in my blood though, I got that same adrenaline rush as if I was playing basketball trying to score the next basket. The main reason I liked selling drugs more than robbing was because I could make three times the money as a dope boy than being a robber. I also was getting into more trouble being a robber. I was constantly running from the police because I didn't want to get caught with a gun. Getting caught with a gun meant major jail time. I eventually did get caught though, three times for possession of a weapon.

SOMETHING DIFFERENT

My first attempt to try something different or as I would like to say, "change my life," was in the year 2006. I was released from the state in the month of March. I had this feeling like I was better than what I was doing and bigger than the city I was living in. I wanted more for myself and for the first time in my life I wanted to do something different.

While incarcerated I thought about finding just one girl, having a kid, and maybe marriage. All the above is something different than how I was used to living or seeing life played out. I went months without selling any type of drug; I was trying my hardest to find jobs and my own apartment; more things that was different than the life I was used to living. I was focused on trying to do the right thing but that curse was riding on my back, pulling me down slowly.

After months of being denied and said no to, I was fed up. My curse got the best of me; I got back into being the person that I thought was over. I thought about all the people that I was close to; friends and family members, and compared our lives to the older ones to see how much our lives were the same. I wasn't surprised at the results I came up with because I'd seen it all my life anyway. Repeat! History always repeats itself. What if I wanted to change so badly but didn't know how to because of what I had been doing for last fifteen years? Like I said this was my first attempt and I know why I failed. "Easier said, than done" is a statement I took for granted.

After my first attempt of changing, I failed miserably and I didn't fail at just my first attempt. I failed again, and again, and again after that. My curse had already worked its magic and did so much damage to my mind and way of life that it felt like it was hard to come back from. But still, I was determined to be a better person. I started to learn from my mistakes and each one of my mistakes was different. Eventually they started to dwindle down. I guess I had made so many mistakes that I just couldn't make any more.

As an adult my criminal activity could no longer be justified. Every man and woman has a mind to consciously make a decision of their own. No matter the odds against you, you still have a decision to make. Me, I chose the easy route but the easy route wasn't my safest route. I was headed for destruction and for the first time, I knew it. Regardless of the decisions I made in the past, I made those choices because I knew how to live with it. Do I regret some my choices? Of course, but who's to say I would've made the same choices if my circumstances were different? What I do know is that today, I have overcome being a statistic. I live life accordingly; I'm not breaking the law, I'm not selling drugs and most of all, I'm still alive to talk about it.

I used to blame my family tree for the reason I did the things that I really didn't want to do. I broke every law a

16

thug could break with the exception of murder/rape or things of that nature. I was caught up in a life time full of deceit, lies, drama, chaos, and lots of death. In order to reverse the way I had become so accustom to living, I had to endure pain to fully understand what true happiness really felt like. I had to have a will to rid all of my pain and do better. I had to get strong for me (first) before I could help others.

Like I said before, the curse is already there, waiting for a single thought to trigger the history and spread like a plague; with the hope of killing you in the process. In the same way negative thoughts, opportunities or people come around let that vibe sit right where it is. Don't let it spark anything. Move forward and never act on impulse. Never give in to becoming a statistic and no matter what you see as a child or how you're brought up, never let up on what you believed in first.

I spent eighteen years of my life as an anti-law abiding citizen. By the time I realized what was happening to my life it was too late, the damage was done. Some of the criminal charges stream all the way back from the year 2001-2005; mistakes that I'm paying for right up to this

17

day. But I'm overcoming it all. To some people I'm still considered doomed because of what I have already done unlawfully and to some I'm an inspiration because of who I am today.

Who I am today is what matters the most and who I'll become tomorrow is what God has in store for me. Change isn't easy nor can I say that it promises instant results but if it's really what you want, don't stop at anything or let anybody tell you otherwise. No matter how it started or how it went you too can reverse the curse!

FROM BROKEN TO BREAKTHROUGH

CHAPTER 2

Tanya O'Brien

"History will continue to repeat itself if you do not identify and acknowledge unhealthy patterns of behavior. The one common denominator I could find through these unhealthy relationships was me."

When I think back to a time and place where this broken and most vulnerable little girl had been stripped of her innocence, I feel sad for her. If I could go back in time, I would tell her not to give up. I would tell her to never mistreat herself; to love herself. I learned that a part of any healing process and the possibility to move forward is to go back and heal the broken child that may very well be living inside of us all.

At the age of seven a child's biggest worry is about playtime; when it starts and why it has to end. However, what was normal for me at seven, can be seen as abuse and neglect to others. Around the age of seven was when I realized that my mother was mentally ill. Remembering the time when my mother's paranoia and fear was poured upon my siblings and I, gave us many sleepless nights. There was not a day that had gone by where my mother hadn't mentioned she was not feeling well and if anything were to happen to her we could find her identification and health insurance cards located in the front of her purse. Can you imagine as a child believing *everyday* was your mother's last day? This behavior is considered emotional abuse and the affects are very damaging to a child's emotional and mental health. A child is supposed to feel loved, protected, supported and safe. Instead I felt sad, afraid, unprotected and not supported.

In my home we hardly ever had food to eat. My mother was depressed and spent the majority of her time either resting on a couch or in a room sleeping. When she was up and moving around she would scream and verbally abuse my siblings and I. We were constantly called inappropriate names and as a child it was very hard not to believe the words she spoke.

As children, my siblings and I did not have a lot of clothes and the very little we had were rarely clean. Our home did not have much furnishing and what we had was broken. For

21

years my mother's mental illness went untreated. My siblings and I were forced into the realization that it would be up to us to take on all the responsibilities if we were going to have a chance to make it.

TAKING RESPONSIBILITY

At the age of twelve and nine, my sister and I did our own food shopping, whenever we could and despite the weather, even in the winter. As two young children walking in winter weather, it was dangerous; especially when you're walking without the proper attire such as a winter coat, gloves, hats and snow boots.

I remember watching my sister calculating the costs of each product put into our carriage. She did her best to make sure we had enough food stamps when it was time to pay. The walk home felt like forever; battling winds and feet of snow while pushing a carriage full of groceries. While we were young, we did what we had to do to survive.

In addition to the groceries, taking care of the house also meant we had chores around the house as well. We would take turns with chores and washed our clothes out by hand just to have clean clothes for school. I remember gathering up the dirty clothes from a closet where the clothes were piled up as high as a mountain and put them in them in the bathroom. Kneeled down in front of the bathtub, I would toss in as many pieces of clothing that I could and began to wash the clothes by hand.

We did not have laundry detergent, we did not have soap and we borrowed toilet tissue from the neighbors on most occasions; when we mustered up enough courage to ask.

A child's very first teacher is their parent, their parents or their caretaker. If a child is being raised by someone who is mentally and emotionally unstable, unfortunately that child will learn and develop unhealthy patterns of behavior which usually leads to poor choices.

As a child, I was not taught proper personal hygiene, I had to learn on my own. No one taught me how to feel comfortable around a boy, let alone a man. Instead, I learned how to use violence to solve problems. I learned how to protect my siblings and my mother and I knew how important it was to keep family business private so that no one; not anyone, knew of our struggles.

A TURN FOR THE WORSE

By the age of fourteen, my life had taken a turn for the worse. I started to date. I had my very first boyfriend and he was nineteen years of age. Within that relationship a lot of my brokenness began to reveal itself. I was an insecure person who had no knowledge of how to have any relationship. So whenever issues arose I began looking for an escape. My reality was too much to deal with. I did not feel good about myself and I just wanted the pain that I was suppressing to go away. At the age of fourteen years old, I was introduced to marijuana and alcohol which gave me the escape I needed, so I thought.

Many of the kids from my neighborhood were already into drinking and getting high so I found myself hanging with them more. The feeling was everything I had been looking for. It was an escape from my reality. It was a numbing sensation. It was as if being under the influence had taken the pain away, even if just for a moment.

Looking back, I remember that I never hid anything from my mother. In a healthy family, this would have been the perfect opportunity for my mother to intervene but she didn't. She couldn't. It was almost like she was living vicariously through me. My mother and I would sit and talk about my drunken stories and fist fights that I had. Or we talked about which female in the neighborhood was talking bad about me.

By the age of sixteen, my older sister and older brother were no longer in the home. They left with the hopes of a better life. I stayed home and was running the streets to the point where I had dropped out of high school. At this time my mother's mental illness seemed to be getting worse and I had already got out of my first relationship and began another one.

I began to date a boy who was new to the neighborhood. This was exciting because he caught the interest of many girls but he only had his eyes set out on me. I was so used to seeing the same old boys that I grew up with; his interest in me was refreshing.

I made it a mission of mine to catch his attention. I would pick out what I thought was a cute outfit. I would do my hair nicely and put on makeup. Once I felt presentable, I would take walks down the street just to see if he would notice me and he did.

The relationship between him and I happened so fast. I never really took the time to get to know him as a person. What I did know was that he came from a large family. Both his mother and one of his sister's rented two separate apartments in my neighborhood. I also noticed that he was selling drugs; his behavior when dealing with strangers who would come to our neighborhood looking for him was a dead giveaway. This type of activity was seen and accepted in my environment because it was our normal way to survive.

I will never forget the first time he hit me. We had been dating for a few weeks and were inseparable. But there were times where he would get jealous. Whether he saw me talking to old friends or wasn't happy with what I was wearing, he showed signs of abuse early on that I just brushed off and assumed it was all because he cared about me.

We started staying with one of his other sister's who was living on the north side of our city. This was the first time that I was away from home and out of my neighborhood. I found myself living the "adult life," although I was left caring for his sister's daughter, cleaning her house and attempting to cook. I had no idea how to care for a child. I was still a child myself.

There were times when company would come to his sister's house. In those times, his demeanor would change and his insecurities would show. He did not want any other guy looking at me or even speaking to me. That is when he decided that it would be better if I just stayed in a bedroom when company would come.

The first time I was sent in the bedroom, I saw a bed, nightstand and one small television. I sat on the bed and he closed the door. When I heard the door shut behind me, I started to feel confused. Directly in front of me there was a bedroom window and the only window in the room. The blinds on the window were down but sunlight crept through the cracks and was able to bring some light into the room. A short time had passed as I just sat and listened to the laughter that was coming from the living room area just outside of the bedroom. I sat reflecting on my life and felt all alone the more I sat there and the more I thought about all that I had been through.

Marijuana smoke was leaking in the bottom of the bedroom door and made me feel aggravated. I started to feel homesick and missed my mother so much. I wanted to be around someone who I felt loved me unconditionally. It was then when I decided that I'd had enough. I made up my mind that I was ready to go home.

As I lay on the bed it seemed like time was passing slowly. At some point it had turned to night. Still, I lay on the bed in complete darkness. I could have got up to turn on the light but I did not want to draw any attention to myself by making any noise. All of a sudden I noticed that everything became quiet. The bedroom door opened and it was him. He looked high and reeked of alcohol but seemed to be smiling and in a good mood. I on the other hand felt angry and fed up but I did not want to let him know it. I let a little time pass mustering up the courage to ask that he bring me home. I didn't want to be the built in babysitter and I did not want to cook for anyone who was taking advantage of me. I did not want to be used for sex at his beckon call and I no longer wanted to sit in a bedroom like a caged bird when company came over. I had enough. So finally, I turned to him said "Can you bring me home?"

He looked as though I had caught him off guard. He stared at me with a look of concern and then confusion. He then asked, "why?" I explained to him that I was really missing my mother and it had been a while since I'd seen her so I just wanted to go home to be with her. The truth was, deep down inside, I could not wait to get away from all of them, especially him.

He was hesitant and it felt like forever for him to agree having tried his best to convince me to stay. But I had already made my decision. "Let's go," he finally said, and I collected my belongings. I felt a huge sigh of relief but on the outside I looked emotionless. I did not want to seem too happy; in case he changed his mind.

We headed to the car. Neither one of us spoke a word. We got in the car, he turned the car on and we drove away. I watched his sister's house get further and further away until I no longer could see it. The further we got away the more I started to feel safe again.

During the ride home he started to ask more questions. He wanted me to answer why I wanted to go home. Again, I explained that I was really missing my mother and wanted to see and spend time with her. It felt like an interrogation. It seemed like no matter what I said it would not be good enough for him. Then he went from just talking to becoming angry. He started yelling and screaming accusations of me wanting to be with other guys, me cheating on him and that I really had plans to leave him. His thoughts were making him enraged. I tried calming him down by continuing to reassure him that I was not leaving him. I made it clear that there was no one else. But his anger and aggression worsened and turned into a full blown melt down. He began to cry while still yelling. I had never seen a guy cry before and I didn't know how to feel about it. I was so confused. Where I come from, crying was a form of weakness. It was unacceptable; especially coming from a boy. He continued on and made me feel bad, almost like I had hurt him. Finally, he started to calm down while wiping his tears with the sleeve of his coat.

More calm then the ride began, we had arrived. He pulled his car into the liquor store parking lot directly in front of a path that led into my neighborhood. Once he stopped the car I was going to get out. But he didn't just stop the car. He parked the car, turned it off and looked at me. There was a moment of silence as he looked over at my hand that had grabbed hold of the handle of the car door. Then he reached out and punched me in my face. I couldn't believe what had just happened. I grabbed the eye where I felt the most pain and burst into tears. He hurt me, badly. I pulled down the mirror to look at my face. Just that quick my face was red and overflowing with tears. My left eye was puffy and began to swell and bruise all at once. A mist the tears, all I could do was blurt out, "Oh My God!"

In a panic, he quickly began apologizing. He was yelling "I didn't mean to hit you but you made me do it!" He told me that there was no way I could go home now because if I did, someone would notice my face and contact the law. He was right. He would get in trouble and he should get in trouble for assaulting me but at that time I was already conditioned to protect anyone who hurt me and that is what I did. I agreed with him. Then, he turned on his car and we drove away.

In that moment, I gave away my power. I felt sad, scared, hopeless and powerless; I now know that an abuser is a weak and insecure person. They will manipulate, cause fear, drain a person's self confidence and in my situation, had figured out how to alienate me from my family and friends. My advice to anyone who may find themselves in an abusive relationship is to tell someone you trust whether it is a family member, friend or neighbor. Please never ever reason with anger. Do not take on other person's problems and make them your own. Do not feel obligated to help others before helping yourself. Being able to identify the red flags can be vital; it can save your life. Red flags are signs of unhealthy behavior such as jealousy, control, manipulation, verbal and physical abuse.

In the weeks and months of just a year's time frame, I suffered so much emotional and physical abuse. I had become pregnant twice and endured two painful miscarriages at the hands of my abuser. I was a prisoner. It felt all too familiar; like being stuck in a house with no food, hot water, lack of clothes and no toiletries.

On my own, I tried escaping several times but every time I did I was caught and the beatings became more brutal. Time had passed and once again he was facing another jail sentence. He had been arrested on many occasions for criminal activity but this time was different. This time he couldn't figure out a way to avoid jail time so I knew this would be my only opportunity to get away. The day he had court I went home. I heard through friends in my neighborhood that he was sentenced to a few years. I had never felt more relieved in my life. I did not and would not have any further contact with him or his family.

When I turned about seventeen, my mother received an eviction notice from our Housing Authority for paperwork not processed on time. My mother had the option to fight the eviction process but chose not to. I was the only one working at the time, but had to quickly figure out where we were going to live. We decided that we were going to rent a room at a local hotel.

This hotel was known to house drug dealers, addicts and prostitutes. Things seemed like they would work out because thankfully my aunt was able to quickly get my mother a job as a bus monitor for the transportation company my aunt drove for. This was the very first time in my entire life I had ever seen my mother work and I was so proud of her. Between my mother and I's paycheck being able to afford renting this room seemed possible, right? The problem was neither my mother nor I had the slightest idea of how to be financially responsible and properly manage money.

33

After spending some time adjusting to our new life and schedule, the overwhelming responsibility of dealing with adult issues had taken a toll on me. I was working long hours and just wanted a break from it all. I needed relief. I was getting to know other residents of the hotel along with the staff. On the first floor of the hotel there was a bar. After a long day of work I spent many nights in the bar drinking and carrying meaningless conversations with the locals. Here I was, seventeen years old with adult responsibilities and an alcohol problem. Eventually I became irresponsible with my money and my mother could no longer depend on me to help cover the cost of renting the room at the hotel. I didn't know it but found out later that my mother reached out to my sister and asked if she could stay with her and my sister said yes. While my mother stayed with my sister, I was bouncing from one house to another sleeping on couches.

My life was a complete mess. I did not have one solid healthy relationship. I continued to abuse my body through drugs, alcohol and promiscuity. The sad part about it all was that I did not care about myself one bit and in return it affected those who loved me.

A NEW DAY

By the time I was eighteen I met a guy through mutual friends. This was around the same time that I was selling drugs just to get by. I was still running the streets, still fighting, riding around in stolen cars, hanging out in local bars and on occasion robbing people that were looking for drugs. This guy had the same characteristics of those that I dated in the past. Here was a guy that was aggressively pursuing me and as much as I initially found no romantic interest in him, I gave in and allowed this relationship to happen. I was not listening to my inner voice or gut instinct. I was a people pleaser. I was someone who craved validation. He made me feel wanted and I liked how that felt.

What attracted me to him was our love for writing and music. Over time I found that our instant connection was based on all we had in common. We both used writing as an outlet. Writing was probably the only method of healthy expression I used at that time. Writing was a form of therapy I discovered at eleven years old.

Unfortunately, in this relationship I had become the abuser. I vowed to myself that no man would ever put his hands on me again without me fighting back or hitting first. Any time there was a disagreement and he made a sudden move I pounced on him. Throughout the relationship, he and I found ourselves in handcuffs. I never realized that I was attracting guys based on how I felt about myself. We all carry energy within ourselves that connect to other people's energy. What I was giving out was coming right back to me. Despite the crazy nature of our relationship, we had our first child just a few years later. While he was incarcerated, I went through the pregnancy and birth of our child without him.

I grew up without a father figure. There were no examples of a man to compare to. But I learned that a father is a man who is tender and caring. A man that is able to express sensitivity around his children. He is attentive and a gentleman. A father is the ultimate protector. I missed out on not having a dad in my life. I needed my dad to care for me, guide me, protect me and most importantly love me.

When you have a history of unhealthy relationships and continue repeating those same patterns of bad behavior and poor choices without intervention and proper treatment this viscous cycle will continue. It becomes a generational curse. History will continue to repeat itself if you do not identify and acknowledge unhealthy patterns of behavior. One common denominator through these unhealthy relationships was me. I was not familiar with what a healthy relationship was. I did not know that I deserved to be treated with respect and that I was worthy of love. I had to learn how to love myself first, flaws and all, in order to be able to love someone else. What I deserved was someone who genuinely had my best interest at heart. I deserved someone who wanted me to be well. I needed a person who could add to my life and not subtract from it.

As the years passed, I found that I was raising my son alone. I was still an addict and my son's father was in and out of jail. My poor choices and behavior continued. I was still working and was able to get my own apartment but I created an unhealthy environment for my son. My son's father and I were off and on within our relationship. Four years later I became pregnant again.

My daughter was born when I was only seven months pregnant and shortly after her birth she was diagnosed with down-syndrome and a heart condition. I initially felt like God was punishing me for all of the bad things that I had done. I now know, God gives you what he knows you can handle and that my daughter was a gift that I so desperately needed in my life. Ten months later, my daughter had open-heart surgery and it was successful.

The following year my mother was diagnosed with terminal cancer. She was not feeling well and after meeting with the doctors, my siblings and I found out that she had six months to a year left to her life. I felt at the time, this was the ultimate blow to my spirit. I could not wrap my head around the fact that my mother was dying. My mother only lived two months after her diagnosis.

After my mother's passing, my addiction spiraled out of control. I had created so many problems with my children's family that they decided to get The Department of Children and Family services involved. A case worker unexpectedly showed up at my home where luckily, I had not yet started drinking for the day. My house was clean. I had food in my fridge and my children appeared to be well taken care of. I was able to convince the worker that this family was vindictive and they only wanted to cause more harm than good. All ties were cut with my children's father's family because I felt like I could not trust them. Shortly after that my children's father went back to jail.

With my children's father back in jail I began having a house full of people that I could get high and drunk with every day. It is also when I started talking to my neighbor.

My neighbor was a lot younger than me and showed a lot of responsibility when it came to helping with my children. I never had that before. We had a lot of the same issues that stemmed from addiction and domestic violence. It was almost normal to have the cops show up to our house because of our fighting or his criminal activity. We got closer and closer until finally I had become pregnant and was expecting my second daughter.

When my daughter turned four months old we decided that we were going to move and create a fresh start for our new family. We moved to a new apartment. We changed locations but nothing other than our address changed; he was being unfaithful and we both were addicts and constantly putting our hands on each other.

One particular morning, I woke up so hung over and noticed that my son missed his bus to school. The guilt that

I was feeling was so overwhelming because I knew I was constantly disappointing my son. I left the girls with their dad and took my son to the library to make up for him missing school. On the way down the street I was drinking a bottle of vodka that was in my coat pocket. I was drunk by the time we reached the library. My son rented some books and we began walking home. On the way home, I could barely walk and had passed out on the lawn of a court house. I was surrounded by the public, lawyers and an ambulance. The ambulance brought my son and I home where I climbed up on my couch and passed out again. When I awoke, my children were being removed from my home. That was the worst day of my life. I had failed my children. The following day I became clear headed and the pain of losing my children was internally destroying me. That same day I decided that I would enter rehab so that I could fight for my life in order to be strong enough to fight to get my children back.

During my visit in rehab I experienced a pivotal moment that would change my life forever. I was in the living room area alone; sitting on one of the chairs looking out of the window. I heard a song playing on the television. It was, *Never would have made it*, by Marvin Sapp. I don't know why this touched my soul the way it did but I stood up and walked toward the television. I watched the video as I began to cry. I cried so heavily. The years of pain that had been pushed down so deep poured out as I begun to release. I have never cried so hard in my life. It was almost like a volcano that had erupted within.

That is when God came into my life. I surrendered to him all that I knew because my life was not working with me being in control. I spent over a month in rehab and upon leaving I entered into an outpatient program. I was feeling physically and mentally healthy. I had learned healthier coping skills and was ready to start a better life. I entered into treatment where I was receiving therapy twice a week; I maintained it for a year. I was having visitation with my children and soon it became overnights where my children came home for the weekend. Ten months later my children were home for good.

I attended Alcoholics Anonymous and Narcotics Anonymous meetings to sustain my sobriety and decided that I would go back to school. So much in my life was changing for the better. I ended my relationship and continued to work on myself from the inside out. I obtained my G.E.D. and went to college. I got my license and bought a car. I spent two years in college and earned a degree in Human Resource Management.

In order to *Reverse the Curse*, I first had to acknowledge the patterns of unhealthy behavior and choices. I needed to identify generational curses that had been passed on; such as addiction, depression, neglect, abuse, manipulation, violence, insecurities, racism, discrimination, mental illness and selfish behavior. Once identified, I needed to figure out how to stop this vicious cycle that would affect the generations coming after me. For my children and I we stress the value in communication. Teaching my children the value of communication will help them to be confident in showing someone how to treat them and verbally express boundaries of what they will and will not accept in their life; a lesson I was never taught.

Reversing the curses in our lives is about respecting yourself enough to not settle for less than you deserve. It is practicing healthy coping skills such as expressive outlets like writing, walking in nature, reaching out to a friend to release bottled up emotions and creating a healthy support system of people who genuinely care about your well being. It is making choices that benefit you, your children or family.

To reverse the curse, is to be conscious and awoke. By allowing God into my life, I no longer felt the absence of a father. God is the ultimate father. He is my protector who is a loving and guiding force in my life. My life is complete because I am happy, my children are thriving and my relationships are healthy. My life is complete because I am reversing the curse.

THE CRACK

SPOT

Jason LaPlanche

"Remember the process of your deliverance; it's painful to deal with dark things. It's not easy addressing what former generations ignored. But the longer it sits, the harder it gets."

I have a spot on my couch that I like to call "the crack spot." The crack spot is the place where you get good and comfortable, where your body and the couch become one and are perfectly aligned; in sync with each other. It's the spot where you sit and the couch automatically complies and feels like it fits you like a glove. One of the things I look forward to the most when I have one of those rare days at home to just chill and relax is to get real comfortable in my crack spot.

There are some unwritten rules about the crack spot; like, don't ask me to do anything that requires me to move, don't touch anything that is touching me, and I'm not sharing. The main one that everybody knows is, don't bother dad while he's on the couch.

45

The plan is to do everything in my power to not have to move again, once I sit down. It's like I'm a kid again, building forts around the house with blankets and chairs and pillows; I build around the crack spot. I change into my house clothes (that shirt with the hole in it, mismatch socks, old shorts) and grab all of the essentials in order for my plan of not moving to become a reality. I grab my beverages (preferably Pepsi), snacks, blanket, a few pillows, a cell phone charger and the most important piece; the TV remote. And in the case that I sit down and realize that I forgot something, I call one of the kids to grab it because the crack spot cannot be neglected for a second!

The truth is we all want to be comfortable in life. Whether you want to be comfortable financially, comfortable in your relationships, comfortable with your weight (hallelujah, holla back), or even comfortable sitting in your favorite spot on the couch, we all want to be comfortable. When it comes to the basic needs of life, being comfortable with who you are and in what you are doing is key in experiencing successful outcomes. However, the crack spot called, "The Comfort Zone," can become the most dangerous place for a progressive person to sit in. Being comfortable has the power and potential to allow laziness to feel welcome. Very often people get comfortable to the point where they unknowingly allow laziness to become a way of life. The crack spot for me is a seemingly harmless place and some might even say it's healthy because we all need "me time." But the problem is, eventually, I'm going to have to get up and do something; like go to the bathroom. Even when I have to go to the bathroom, it's hard to get up from the crack spot because I'm so comfortable. I'll try to hold it as long as I can just so that I don't have to move and deal with the agony of being uncomfortable. Sometimes, when a person gets too comfortable, they may start trying to find ways to accomplish their goal without "getting up."

Generational curses work the same way. There's a point where someone in your family that you most likely have never met, had an issue and began to settle in their sin. They became really comfortable in a weak area and instead of addressing it; they decided to allow it to become their "crack spot." It's their place of comfort, rest and familiarity. They build around it, they made life decisions around it, they try to mask it, and they make excuses for it defending the fact that a curse even exists.

The lie of generational curses is that they deceive you into believing the curse is who you are. It tries to get you to accept the lie of familiarity as identity so that you get comfortable functioning in dysfunction and being dysfunctional becomes your norm. When a person begins to embrace this place in their lives for too long, it becomes a way of life. It makes getting up a difficult option because any move outside of this place is painful and uncomfortable. The sad truth is that it may have even become apparent to others around them, but nobody wanted to say anything and it developed into the family secret that wasn't so secret. Generation after generation after generation, this unresolved issue, secret sin, mama's messes and daddy's demons, start to become a part of the characteristics of the family. Since nobody wants to address it, deal with it or even talk about it, it becomes part of the DNA of your life. By the time it gets to you, you just thought it was the way you were and becomes a familiar friend!

Like many things, people often choose to be bound in the familiar than to be free in the uncomfortable. Demons/strongholds are assigned and don't leave their assignment; they have to be dismissed. For example, in Mark chapter 5, Jesus arrives at the cemetery where there is a demon possessed cutter. He runs to Jesus and asks him what's going on and why is he there to terrorize him. Jesus asks his name and the man is silent but the demon(s) speaks through the man and says, "We are legion, for we are many." Jesus then casts out the demons from the man into the pigs. The man was then freed, fully clothed and in his right mind. The point is demons are always looking for a host. It's not possible for them to be active in the earth without a "sponsor." My point is not so much about demon possession as it is about spirits staying in a region, a family or a person. They are assigned and have no intention of leaving their assignment. That's why you can see the same struggles down your family line; strongholds must be broken, NOT bartered with.

For the majority of my early years, I grew up in a home with four women; my mom, grandmother (Smitty) and two aunts; with occasional random visits by my uncle. My dad wasn't in the home, he was a military veteran stationed on the other side of the United States. Although he wasn't in the home, he was always in my life. So growing up, the ladies in my life wanted to ensure that I wasn't "soft" they did their best to teach me to be a man as best as they could as women.

One of the funny life lessons that I was raised under being an 80's baby was, "you better not come home crying." What was implied is that if you get into a fight, don't let anyone beat you up and you come home crying about it; be a man, fight back and wipe your face! Another one was, "don't let nobody put their hands on you." What was implied is, don't let anyone hit you and you don't hit back; good ol' eye for an eye. Now these were just two of the many lessons I learned growing up, but what I wasn't aware of is that in my family there were generations of people with serious anger issues and no one addressing them in me. My dad, who was on the other side of the country not really having to deal with my everyday development stuff, didn't get to see in me the things that he saw in himself. So, while on the outside it looks like I'm just getting into fights and having these "little" problems, nobody was addressing what was already at work on the inside. These "demons were developing" and I embraced the anger as my identity. I was a good kid with a short fuse because "I don't take no mess," not realizing that there's a spirit that's attached to me, that others in my family had. I was dealing with something that no one wanted or knew how to deal with. Just like other generations, I learned how to deal with it and stay in my "crack spot" so that I didn't have to deal with the agony of uncomfortable. Let's be honest, who wants to deal with this stuff anyways, "if I ain't broke, don't fix me," "I'm fine the way I am," "whoever is really for me will love and accept me just like I am," or in the words of Drake, "No new friends;" I used to think all of that. Here's the issue, I have children and whatever is unresolved in me, becomes an issue for them; *what I don't allow to die in me, will develop in them.* When I began to see at an early age in them, some of the same qualities in me that needed to be broken, I decided it was time to get off the couch.

Now, I must warn you, you can be saved and still have a "crack spot." These generational curses are not necessarily heaven or hell issues but they are life issues. I truly accepted Jesus as Lord at 19 years old, but did not even begin to "deal with my demons" until the age of 27. So here are some of the things that will help you get off of the couch and leave "the crack spot," in your life.

YOU HAVE TO WANT TO GET UP
No one can want change for you. Anything in your life that's going to change starts with your desire for change. It's important to have a relationship with Jesus Christ because it's Him that gives you the will and desire to get

off the couch (Philippians 2:13). You will never want to on your own; we love our darkness and make excuses for our issues, but when we allow the Lord Jesus to come into our hearts and be Lord in our lives, our desires drastically change. We begin to see life from a different lens and what we were once comfortable in we no longer fit. Getting off the couch was always possible, but because I had no desire, all I used was excuses and I got comfortable in "my spot." I realize that no matter how much anyone called me or what happened in the house, I wasn't getting off of that couch until I was ready. Anything that caused me to have to get up, I would call someone else to do. When I began to see that I was calling people to do what I was supposed to get up and do, it changed my life. Destiny starts with a decision. Your life on earth can and will begin to change when you're ready to get up. Generational curses can be broken but the desire must be greater than the demon.

YOU CANNOT GET UP ALONE

Jesus got up so you can get up. *"The Spirit of God, who raised Jesus from the dead, lives in you. Just as God raised Christ Jesus from the dead, he will give life to your mortal bodies by this same Spirit living within you,"* Romans 8:11.

You can have a desire but not have a deliverer. Make no mistakes about it, if this were a self-help book I would have left it at point 1, desire. But desire alone is not enough, it's the starting point. Now, with this new desire you need someone who has the ability to help deliver you because you can't deliver yourself. Part of the good news of the gospel is not just that Jesus died for you, but he is now alive in you. So with that desire He also brings a power to your life that you never had and could never have without His Spirit (Acts 1:8). Curses live through comfort-ability, but freedom comes through an active faith in Christ.

HE GETS YOU UP TO KEEP YOU UP

One of the biggest mistakes we make is thinking that deliverance happens and that's it. You can be delivered in a moment, boom! Just like that. But sanctification; being set apart to be used by God in a special way, is a process. So when God delivers you, it's for you to stay delivered. Sometimes we get so excited about the initial experience that we neglect the continual process and it is possible that once God gets you up, you can sit back down. *"So Christ has truly set us free. Now make sure that you stay free, and don't get tied up again in slavery to the law,"* Galatians 5:1.

What Paul challenges us with here, is to make sure that we *stay* free; that we don't go back to "the crack spot;" that place in your life that is comfortable and familiar. Being free from generational curses is about more than getting a one-time fix. It is a lifelong commitment to a lifestyle of freedom.

Some of the best ways to stay off of the couch is to remember the pain of getting up. Remember the process of your deliverance. It's painful to deal with dark things. It's not easy addressing what former generations ignored and the longer it sits the harder it gets! Always keep in mind your scars so that you remember what you had to endure. Scars tell us two things; (1) that something came against you (2) that you conquered what came!

Jesus is the only one that has the power to cancel any curse. *"But Christ has rescued us from the curse pronounced by the law. When he was hung on the cross, he took upon himself the curse for our wrongdoing. For it is written in the Scriptures, Cursed is everyone who is hung on a tree,"* Galatians 3:13.

Everything He did in the flesh was an example of what He can do in our flesh if we surrender ourselves to Him. His desire is for you to live in freedom; not to be free from him but to be free in Him. Now is your time to end the generational curse and create a generational blessing.

THE PRIORITY
OF PRAYER

CHAPTER 4

Lakeisha S. Powe

"What we say is a part of the process of prayer but it's what's in our hearts that speaks the loudest."

For generations within my family I watched the unwed live as though they were wed. When I was young I didn't question it. I actually thought it was normal behavior. As I matured and became a believer I found out that this was not the design that God set for our lives. God designed it so that male and female would wed and become one flesh; to marry, be fruitful, and multiple.

Other common repeated behavior includes alcohol abuse, drug abuse, teen pregnancy, anger management issues, and physical abuse, some of which may have been more familiar to you. For me, couples' living like they were married, even though they weren't, was the one recurring behavior that I could relate to the most with. You might have felt just as I did in thinking the recurring behavior was normal. When this is all you have seen it's hard to see things differently. Romans 12:2 tells us to be transformed by the renewing of our minds. When your mind is renewed you can began to see things differently. You can begin to see that what was once considered as normal is no longer normal.

I have experienced a time in my life where prayer was not the norm, nor was it a priority. The only time I prayed was when I was in need of something or wanted to be rescued from a thing. I would pray and expect an immediate response from God. I felt like, "Hey it's ME, Lakeisha Powe, your daughter standing in the need of prayer." Isn't that how prayer works? What else should I have expected? I felt like I deserved a quick answer. I wanted God to drop what He was doing and whoever else He was helping and turn all His attention to me. I was selfish like that. The motives of my prayers were a result of my selfishness.

Prayer was the last resort in correcting all my mess ups, bad decisions, and outright disobedience. I operated in this manner for a while because I didn't understand the priority and power of prayer. What I learned the hard way was that prayer should not have been a last resort but something I needed to be doing as my first pursuit in all matters of my life; good or bad.

In preparation of reading this chapter, pray this prayer with me: "God I ask that you would so kindly open up my heart as I prepare myself to develop a firm understanding regarding prayer. I surrender to the guidance of the Holy Spirit. In Jesus name, Amen.

You have just prayed a very simple yet powerful prayer. It is important to understand that no matter how short or long your prayers are, they still hit the ears of God.

THE PROCESS OF PRAYER

What we say is a part of the process of prayer but it's what's in our hearts that speaks the loudest. Our hearts should be in a posture that is pure in motive as it relates to prayer. Our only motive in prayer should not be to gain but to be obedient. Jesus taught his disciples through a parable instructing them that they should always pray and not give up (Luke 18:1-8). In this moment in scripture, Jesus expressed the importance of prayer even when things are difficult. The same applies today. It is important to pray in the same manner; praying day and night and in good or bad times.

God is all powerful and all knowing. He knows your prayers before you even pray them. Although He is aware of your needs and desires before you ask, praying activates your faith and exercises the amazing privilege that God provides in being able to communicate with Him. Prayer builds your relationship to trust God more, hear more clearly and more easily follow his direction. Obedience to prayer shows that your faith lies in God's ability to do exceedingly, abundantly, and above all we can ask and think (Ephesians 3:20, 21).

Knowing God's word is also a part of the process of prayer. When you are able to implement His word in your prayer you can rest assure that you are praying with power. God responds to His word. This does not mean that you need to have the bible memorized front and back in order to pray; however it is good to have some key scriptures written down or hidden in your heart and ready to grab when you pray. For example 1 John 1:9 is a verse of scripture that I remind myself of daily. This scripture talks about the power of confession. God is not like your best friend Sally who holds a grudge. He wants to forgive. Confessing your faults before God frees your heart to stand pure in motive before God, even in prayer.

The bible declares in James 5:16 to "Confess your faults one to another, and pray one for another, that ye may be healed. The effectual fervent prayer of a righteous man availeth much." Notice the first portion of this scripture "confess your faults one to another." Parallel to the 1 John scripture above, this text also amplifies the need for confession in prayer. This scripture is one of the beautiful reminders of God's faithfulness. If ever you are out of alignment with His word just confess and He will forgive.

So often, people tend to overlook the confession of sin. The reality is we are human and we all have sin. Not *had* but we *have* sin in our lives. Before any prayers are sent up we must first confess our sins and not only confess but confess in a manner of repentance. Yes, *repentance is a part of the prayer process too!*

As you approach God in prayer confess your sins and ask God to forgive you of your sin. Confession is required of the believer. Who is the believer? The believer is the one that repents of their sin, acknowledges that Jesus is Lord, believes in their heart, and confesses with their mouth that Jesus Christ died on the cross for our sins, was buried in the tomb, and that on the third day God raised Him from the dead (Romans 10:9). Like Jesus, the life of a believer requires a willingness to do die to self-daily and live a life according to the instructions provided in the Word of God. His instructions are most important in your daily walk.

Another scripture you can use when you pray is Matthew 6:6. This passage points to personal prayer time. Our personal time in prayer is just as essential as our corporate prayer time. For your personal prayer time, find a secret place, close the door and talk to God. You may have heard the song sung in church that says "Have a little talk with Jesus. Tell him all about your troubles…" This is song is a testament to God being available and always listening to the matters of your heart. Creating a special place for your personal prayer time allows you to express yourself thoroughly. When you pray, you don't have to worry about who is listening or watching; it's just you and God. I'm reminded of the movie, *War Room*, TriStar, 2015, and how the woman in the story set up her prayer area in an actual closet with scripture reminders and prayer requests posted on the wall. The reality is you can do the same. Do whatever it takes for you to get to your private place of prayer.

PRAYING WITH PURE MOTIVE

As I stated above the posture of your heart is what matters most in prayer. Prayers are most effective when you pray with sincerity and a surrendered spirit. Only you and God truly know the condition of your heart, just like He did with Samuel when David was chosen as king. When God sent Samuel into Jesse's house to appoint a new king, Samuel paid attention to the outer appearance of Jesse's sons. The Lord had to make it clear to Samuel that He doesn't look at the things we look at as humans. People may look at the outer appearance but God looks at the heart. Had God left it up to Samuel to appoint the new king he would have chosen a king based on his looks and not his heart, as God was leading him to do. God is just as concerned with our hearts as He was with Samuel and also David's heart.

David was to be the king not based upon his stature; he was a scrawny young boy, but based upon his heart (1 Samuel 16:7). God hears and knows your heart. What an amazing ability! When you think about the matters of your heart and know that there is only ONE that can see what really matters to your heart; the secrets, the lies, the hopes, and dreams, it demonstrates how trustworthy God is. He is

63

trustworthy to not only hold your heart but to help it, clean it and purify it - and that is pretty amazing.

To maintain a pure motive when you pray, check your heart daily. Remain sincere in your motives when you pray. Additionally keep in mind that when you pray you are surrendering your spirit to Him; your total will to Him, "not my will by thine will be done" (Luke 22:42). A pure motive in heart will strengthen you in prayer when praying for yourself, your needs, and the needs of others.

In the past, I misunderstood prayer but you have an opportunity not to. You have an opportunity to change the course of your life; reverse the curse and live out the abundant life God has in store for you, which starts with making prayer a priority. The start of that opportunity is remembering the command to love your neighbor as yourself (Matthew 19:19).

FEVERENT PRAYER

Praying for your neighbor is more than praying about the person who lives next door. Your neighbor is whoever is in your surroundings at the moment. Your neighbor is the person that comes to mind at any given time of the day.

You might be thinking, "How will I have time to pray for others, when I need prayer myself?" Praying for others is not as hard as you think.

One of the ways to start extending your prayers to others is by creating a list. You might create a list for your groceries, chores, bills, etc., why not a prayer list? You never know what someone else is going through. There may be so many around you crying out daily for an answer to their circumstance. They may be saying, Why me? What am I going to do? Why did I have to get cancer? Where am I going to get money to finance my education? Why did my loved one have to die? Why, Why, Why? Even on social media many are really just crying out for help by a power only God can provide. Take time to write down every need of your neighbors and when you go to pray pull the list out and cry out to God on their behalf. You may not know their exact need but God does. In God's power, your prayers can help someone change their life.

The ending of James 5:16 says, "The effectual fervent prayer of a righteous man availeth much." According to the Webster dictionary the word *effectual* means successful in producing a desired result; effective. When you pray you are looking for your prayers to be effective. Prayers are effective only through the power God. In other words when you pray, you pray by and through the power of the Holy Spirit. It is in that power your prayers become effective. Nothing within us produces answered prayers. God and God alone holds the power to answer prayers.

One of the things that brings me great joy is seeing my children with their father. I grew up without my father in the home and without a consistent male role model in my life; I never saw fatherhood defined. I had no definition of what it meant to have a father in my life. My husband is the total opposite with our children. As I watched true fatherhood being defined in my children's lives it provided a definition of how a father truly cares for his children.

When a father is performing in his role as God ordained, it sets order for his children to follow. When that order is followed, it brings the father joy. As it is in the natural it is in the spiritual. When God sees his children holding up the order He has laid out for them, according to the scriptures, it brings Him glory. So whenever you pray, God gets the glory because He set the order.

Also according to the Webster dictionary the word fervent in this passage is having or displaying a passionate intensity. *Developing an intensified passion for prayer is a part of the prayer process.*

Developing a passion for prayer makes it easier to pray and pray more often. Passion is what drives most people to work hard and to do more.

When I started my transportation business many years ago; along with my husband, in order for it to grow we had to be intentional and intense. It was our desire to make sure we stood out from the many companies already operating in our town. We were sure to make our vehicles look different our logo look different and I ran around town making sure our name, "PoweFolk Transportation," was in eyesight for all to see. Our passion to build this business was intense because we wanted success. No one starts a business and doesn't do everything in their power to make it successful. The same applies to making prayer a priority. If you want success in your prayer life, and if you want your prayers to be heard and if you want your prayers to be answered, according to God's will, you have to be intentional with God and intense in your passion to pray.

In addition to drive, passion in prayer is about vulnerability. As a married woman, there is a passion that I have for my husband and no one else. With this passion I am able to be vulnerable with him and share with him my deepest thoughts. Submitting yourself to prayer will allow for this same type of open, honest vulnerability with God. In your most intimate, passionate and vulnerable moment with God you can safely express your inner most hurts, request, doubts, and fears. You can also express your deepest joy, love, and desires to Him.

Finally Paul states "the prayer of a righteous man availeth much." Paul makes the posture of the heart when you pray very clear in this passage. He urges that one must be a 'righteous' man. To be righteous simply means that you be in right standing with God. This is why repentance is so important. When you confess your sins and seek God for forgiveness, you are forgiven and that forgiveness puts you in right standing with God. When a 'righteous' man prays, it brings about restoration, healing, deliverance, and so much more. When you pray with a postured heart, you exercise your faith in God; holding fast to the fact that His word is true. When you pray, believe that He hears your cries, cares about your struggles and is faithful to provide you with the answers you need. So my brother and sister, "Cast thy burden upon Jehovah, and He will sustain thee: He will never suffer the righteous to be moved," (Psalms 55:22). He is for those who believe. And if you believe, your prayers will avail!

Through continued prayer and learning God's word you will begin to see that your normality may have been created around a worldview instead of a biblical view. A world view makes the unmoral seem normal. A world view can define things as right that God says is clearly wrong; including the patterns of life around you. The good news is that these patterns, no matter how familiar, can be broken through the power of prayer.

When God awakens His truth in you, it helps you to understand the life He desires for you to live on this earth. God sent His son Jesus to die for the sins of man, that we might have life and have it more abundantly. Abundant life does not look the same for everyone in that not all will be rich and have fancy cars. Abundant life is freedom from bondage, freedom from fear and freedom from the familiar negative behaviors that run ramped in families today.

Take a moment to look at the patterns within your family. Try to point out the areas that seem to be destructive to the generations before and consider the ones after you. Once you have pinned an issue or a series of issues, you can begin the process of breaking that particular cycle in your family; through prayer.

The saints used to say, "Prayer is the key and your faith unlocks the door." What a truthful declaration. Prayer and faith in God is a combination that anyone can use in the ring of breaking cycles. Are you a fighter? Are you looking to fight on behalf of your family so that your children and their children will not have to fight the same fight? Will you allow this pattern to continue to destroy your family? Will you make the sacrifice on your knees? Will you say enough is enough, something has got to give? Or will you give in and allow ungodly patterns to continue and be the template for the next generation?

Just as God had a plan for the children of Israel He has a plan for you and your family. His words to the children of Israel ring loud as I write this. He says to them, "*For thus saith the LORD, That after seventy years be accomplished at Babylon I will visit you, and perform my good word toward you, in causing you to return to this place. For I know the thoughts that I think toward you, saith the LORD, thoughts of peace, and not of evil, to give you an expected end." Jeremiah 29:10-11.* There is an active plan in place for your life and God is working. Even in the midst of the patterns taking place and it will all work for the good. If you're ready to do the work let's do it!

So as you journey through life, breaking the cycles, barriers, and spiritual strongholds of your family line, make prayer an essential part.

Let us pray.

Father God, we are your people. We the righteous come before you with the reverence and honor we believe is due to you. Father, first and foremost we would like to say thank you. Thank you for being all we need. For we know that all we need, we can find in you. You have laid out instructions in your word pertaining to our lives and one instruction you have given is that we should always pray.

Father we ask that you will provide us with the discipline that is necessary to keep this command in the forefront of our minds. Father we desire not to disappoint you but to fulfill every command that you have requested of us. We thank you that you are not a God of a first, second, or even third chance but that you are a God of many chances. So father, we now ask that you will forgive us. 1 John 1:9 states "If we confess our sins, He is faithful and righteous to forgive us our sins, and to cleanse us from all unrighteousness." So Father on this day please forgive us for all of our sins and cleanse us from all of our unrighteousness.

Father we repent for every relative connected to our family ancestry who may have deliberately or without spiritual wisdom sinned against you. Father we pray that even our body responds to your will. Align every cell, DNA strand and molecular structure to the divine order of destiny our lineage is supposed to represent.

We ask that you provide comfort to those that are grieving and healing for those that are sick. We ask that you would mend the broken hearted as only you can. Father we pray that every generational curse and their manifestations of dysfunction, mental illness, ungodly beliefs, traditions, rituals, perversion, failed marriages, impure motives, flaws, financial and spiritual poverty, oppression, depression or whatever way a curse has manifested itself in our families, be broken off now in the name Jesus. By the blood of Jesus Christ, we command every root of these curses to be uprooted and destroyed.

Father we surrender our lives to you totally and submit our wills to you completely. Father we pray that you will draw those that know you closer to you; that our faith will continually be strengthened.

Father we pray also for the unbeliever; that they will believe that you are the way, the truth and the life and we understand that no one comes to the you, the Father, but through your Son, Jesus. Father we ask that you will draw them to you that they might believe and receive all that you have awaiting them, which is eternal life.

We are so grateful that in you death does not exist but we shall live forever with you in paradise. Father we rest with assurance that your will, will be done. Amen!

HOW DO
I REVERSE

THE CURSE

LIFE AFTER PRAYER

". . .no matter what has happened in your life or your blood line, you are responsible for the choices and decisions you make. If you really want to be free, you will accept that responsibility."

What happens after the prayer, after the tears have dried and the church doors are closed? What do you do then? To understand the impact of your next steps, it is important to first check your level of expectation.

When God created the earth, his level of expectation to envision and command, brought forth change. When He said, "Let there be light," there was light (Genesis 1:3). He did not say, "It's kind of dark around here, maybe there should be light." No! He commanded change to come forth and expected the response of light to shine bright over all the earth, after He spoke it. Without doubts, without hesitation God knew light; the ability to see, would establish the foundations of the earth. When thinking about how you will establish living the rest of your life in a reversed curse state you must command and expect with the same authority. When you do, God responds with signs, wonders and the miracle of generational freedom.

Upon completing this book, "the light" is on, shining bright over the dark areas, secrets and hidden places of your generational lineage. So then, what are you going to envision command and expect in your own life, from this moment forward? What new path will your generation and the generation after establish as a foundation?

In today's culture, even Christians need to be freed from curses spoken against them before they were saved, or from curses that have come upon them through their involvement of willful rebellion (Deuteronomy 29:24-28).

Willful rebellion is simply, "breaking covenant." Breaking covenant leaves holes in your soul for the enemy to trap you into engaging in familiar cursed behaviors. Even when Paul wrote to "not give the devil any foothold, or a place" (Ephesians 4:27), he was writing to Christians! So then, it is important to recognize that curses can work against Christians if they are in rebellion, out of the will of God, or not walking in faith and love. However, whether you are a

Christian or not, here's what you can do to start to reverse the generational curse(s) in your life.

#1 RECOGNIZE THE CURSE EXISTS

The familial patterns of behavior that you noticed when reading this book are not coincidental. They are God's way of showing you the ungodly habits that are deteriorating the blessings due to you and your family. You have to be able to admit you have a problem. That sounds simple, but today's living reflects a day and age of denial. But no matter what has happened in your life or your blood line, you are responsible for the choices and decisions you make. If you really want to be free, you will accept that responsibility.

#2 BREAK THE CURSE

To reverse the pattern of the curse, you need to break it. This, you cannot do by yourself. You can try, but you will indeed fail in every relationship, business endeavor, and with life itself because the ability to truly change from within does not exist without God.

As you apply God's word and power to your life, and as you choose to walk in righteousness and obedience to God, the chains of generational bondage will be broken.

Perhaps you've had multiple affairs, can't seem to stop doing drugs or excessively drinking alcohol, or perhaps you are depressed and it is taking over your life. Breaking the fruit of those curses (those behaviors) start with you reaching out for help. Finding the help you need, will help you get to the root of your issue; the curse. Reach out, connect, and get connected to those who can assist your growth in that direction.

#3 REPLACE THE CURSE

"When an evil spirit comes out of a person, it goes through dry places looking for a place to rest. But it doesn't find any. Then it says, 'I'll go back to the home I left.' When it comes (again), it finds the house swept clean and in order. Then the spirit goes and brings along seven other spirits more evil than itself. They enter and take up permanent residence there. In the end the condition for that person is worse than it was before," Luke 23-27.

As stated earlier in the book, an evil spirit needs a host to survive. So how do you sweep your house clean of negative generational behaviors yet build generational inheritance at the same time? You do it by filling your space and time with new behaviors, new attitudes and new language that speaks life. In Christ you can be a new person, with new relationships and a new perspective. Therefore replacing the curse is about aligning your words and behaviors with the expectations of heaven; even if it means creating new ones.

#4 ACCEPT & RELEASE THE POWER OF LOVE

To become a person (and generation) whose life is transformed by the love of God, you must not only get rid of what holds you captive and keeps you in bondage, but you must also be filled up with love; for God, for self and for others. And to be filled up enough to give love; unconditional love to others, you must first accept it from God.

Here's a secret, unconditional love releases blessing. When God loves on you, He releases the blessing of indescribable peace, despite your past or current circumstances. God never intended or designed your life to be the way it may have turned out thus far; at the point you can choose differently. The good news is that this is not your end. As a matter of fact He brought you here (to this moment, this place, to read this book) to know you make a difference; you are a difference maker for real. God loves you so much that He broke the curse of death with his bloodshed on the cross which frees you from being bound by habitual behaviors, chemical reactions, or negative mindsets that torment your future; you are not obligated to them. Your only obligation is to accept the love and life God has in store for you concerning generational wealth and spiritual abundance.

#5 WALK IT OUT DAILY

Please know that the journey never stops. You do not wrestle against flesh and blood; your mother, father, sister, brother, cousin, aunty, best friend, drinking buddy, supplier, perpetuator, abuser, hater and the like. The battle is spiritual and is God's to fight. The key is to let Him; not trying to make any changes in your own power.

In order to break free from generational curses and walk in freedom, you must learn to walk in obedience to God's ways. It's not about being perfect and without mistakes, it's about a surrendered heart that is pliable toward God. A heart that will get back up and keep trying no matter how difficult the pattern they're trying to break.

Every day is a new day to move forward in discovering the great things God has in store for your blood line that will start to flow from your decision to do something different. In case you were not aware, there is a miracle on the other side of your obedience to stick with the process and let God change your life, your lineage and your destiny.

Remember the devil is the fallen one - HE HAS NO POWER OVER YOU. Yes he's real and can make things look impossible, but you have power over him; with no need to fear. So those thoughts of, "what if I can't," "what if I fail," "what if I lose friends," are just darts from the enemy not wanting you to change. The truth is your impossible situation, feelings, and years of generational defeat are possible to overcome with God because God is on your side.

As you use your spiritual authority over generational behavioral patterns of perversion, ignorance, and destruction, nothing will stop you. You will have power over all curses through the Lord, Jesus Christ. Spend every moment using that power to reverse the curse.

ACKNOWLEDGEMENTS

First and most important I would love to give thanks to God. Thanks for allowing me to use my knowledge to help and give understanding to others; for giving the strength to open up my mind. Second I want to show appreciation to my wife for letting me have the time to myself to focus. You push me to my full potential to be the best man I could be; thanks to you I was able to get peace of mind. Thanks lovey! Last is for the person who made all of this possible, the other person who also pushes me to be great and all I can be, Yolanda Lewis! Thank you for giving me this opportunity to be amazing, great, awesome, and most of all successful. You made a dream come true, so once again thanks big sis!

Garrin J. Mason

Father-God, I thank you for yet another opportunity. I know, without you none of this would be possible. I thank you for never leaving me whether in my time of darkness or when I saw the light. You have guided, supported and loved me and in return allowed me to be a vessel. Through example, I now understand the journey you laid before me.

I thought I was a fatherless child but as an adult, I now know I have the ultimate protector, supporter and loving father; the most high. Thank you, Father-God.

I would also like to thank the incredible Yolanda Lewis for being a friend, mentor and sister. A big thanks to my family especially my children. Mama would have never fought as hard as I have if it weren't for you three blessings that I was gifted with. Thanks to my sister's Anita and Liza for your love and unconditional support. Last but not least, thank you to the teacher's who believed and encouraged me. Mrs. Roberta, I love you.

Tanya O'Brien

To God be the glory! Thanking God for the opportunity to share the gospel through pen and paper. Thank you to my #1 supporter my husband, Daymione Powe; you're awesome! Thank you for always pushing me to be all that God has designed me to be and your continued support during the process. Thank you to my wonderful children for your love and support! I pray that I always remain a Godly example in your lives.

Lakeisha S. Powe

Thank you Jesus for rescuing me from my dark past. I'm still overwhelmed by Him saving me over 17 years ago. He's the reason I don't look like what I've been through. I want to thank my wife (Sharae) for your continued love, support, partnership and motivation when I am at my worst. You continue to push me to be great, challenging me and never allowing me to settle for anything less than greatness! The #SensationalSix #LaPlancheTribe (Kyree, Jediah, Jaiden, Kyla, Jordyn & Jeremiah) I love you guys so much, you are my world, my joy, my heart and I'm privileged to be your dad. You all push me to "get off the couch," literally and figuratively.

I wouldn't be who I am without you all, MY FAMILY: Mom (LaVerne Crayton), Dad (Eddie "Step Out" LaPlanche), Bro's (David "MAK" Thompson, Eddie "Mooky" LaPlanche, Lance Crayton, Devin Crayton) Sis' (VerNece Smith, Rachel LaPlanche), Smitty (Arlene Smith), Nennen (Edith LaPlanche), Aunt's (Victoria Dozier & LaVette Smith) and Uncle (Victor Smith) ... all of my cousins and friends who have become my family. Special thank you to every #Motivator for being a part of this journey with me.

Jason LaPlanche

God does all things well.

I am thankful for each author. The time and passion poured into every page made the book complete. It was an honor to serve you in this capacity. Thank you for laboring with me on this project. May God be glorified!

To my wonderful children, thank you for supporting mommy, always. I love you both incredulously.

To my amazing husband, you hold my heart. I treasure your love and thank you for your guidance and endless support for all of my "bright ideas." You're truly the best.

Yolanda Lewis

REFERENCES

Gallagher, J. (2013). Memories pass between generations. BBC-Health. Retrieved from: http://www.bbc.com/news/health-25156510

Hurley, D. (2015). Grandma's experiences leave a mark on your genes. Discover Magazine May 2013. Retrieved from: http://discovermagazine.com/2013/may/13-grandmas-experiences-leave-epigenetic-mark-on-your-genes

Schmidt, C. W. Uncertain inheritance transgenerational effects of environmental exposures. Environ Health Perspect 121, A298–303 (2013).

Tollervey, J. R. & Lunyak, V. V. *Epigenetics: judge, jury and executioner of stem cell fate. Epigenetics* 7, 823–840, 10.4161/epi.21141 (2012).

Wutz, A. & Jaenisch, R. *A shift from reversible to irreversible X inactivation is triggered during ES cell differentiation. Mol Cell* 5, 695–705. (2000).

Seong, K. H., Li, D., Shimizu, H., Nakamura, R. & Ishii, S. *Inheritance of stress-induced, ATF-2-dependent epigenetic change. Cell* 145, 1049–1061, 10.1016/j.cell.2011.05.029 (2011).

Ebrahim, S. Epigenetics: the next big thing. International Journal of Epidemology (2012)41(1) doi:10.1093/ije/dys015

Sen, A., Heredia, N., Senut, M., Land, S., Hollocher, K., Xiangyi, L., Dereski, M., Ruden, D.M. Multigenerational epigenetic inheritance in humans: DNA methylation changes associated with maternal exposure to lead can be transmitted to the grandchildren. Scientific Reports (5) 14466 (2015). Doi:10.1038/srep14466

Groom, A., Elliot, H.R., Embleton, N.D., Relton, C.L. Epigenetics and child health: basic principles. Archives of Diseas in Childhood. (2010). Doi:10.1136/adc.2009.165712

Pecinka, A. & Scheid, O.M. Stress-Induced Chromatin changes: a critical view on their heritability. Oxford Journals. (2012). Volume 53(5) 801-808. Doi:10.1093/pcp/pcs044

Bible Gateway. American *Standard Version*. Bible Gateway. Web. February 2016.

Bible Hub. American *Standard Version*. Bible Hub. Web. February 2016.

Dictionary. Dictionary.com. Web. February 2016.

Made in the USA
Middletown, DE
10 June 2016